Instant Sublime Text Starter

Learn to efficiently author software, blog posts, or any other text with Sublime Text 2

Eric Haughee

BIRMINGHAM - MUMBAI

Instant Sublime Text Starter

Copyright © 2013 Packt Publishing

All rights reserved. No part of this book may be reproduced, stored in a retrieval system, or transmitted in any form or by any means, without the prior written permission of the publisher, except in the case of brief quotations embedded in critical articles or reviews.

Every effort has been made in the preparation of this book to ensure the accuracy of the information presented. However, the information contained in this book is sold without warranty, either express or implied. Neither the author, nor Packt Publishing, and its dealers and distributors will be held liable for any damages caused or alleged to be caused directly or indirectly by this book.

Packt Publishing has endeavored to provide trademark information about all of the companies and products mentioned in this book by the appropriate use of capitals. However, Packt Publishing cannot guarantee the accuracy of this information.

First published: January 2013

Production Reference: 1220113

Published by Packt Publishing Ltd.
Livery Place
35 Livery Street
Birmingham B3 2PB, UK.

ISBN 978-1-84969-392-9

www.packtpub.com

Credits

Author
Eric Haughee

Reviewer
Ben Selby

Acquisition Editor
Usha Iyer

Commissioning Editor
Priyanka Shah

Technical Editor
Varun Pius Rodrigues

Project Coordinators
Priya Sharma
Esha Thakker

Proofreader
Aaron Nash

Production Coordinator
Prachali Bhiwandkar

Cover Work
Prachali Bhiwandkar

Cover Image
Manu Joseph

About the Author

Eric Haughee is a recent graduate from the University of Tennessee at Chattanooga where he received a Bachelor's degree in Computer Science with a concentration in Application Design. During his time in college, he worked as an intern with companies doing .NET development, PHP development on the LAMP stack, and .NET Pocket PC development. Throughout this time, Eric worked as a contractor using technologies such as PHP and jQuery mobile. Upon graduating, he took a position at JP Morgan Chase as an Application Developer and currently works with .NET technologies. Outside of work, Eric dabbles in Ruby, Python, and other technologies for web and application development. He currently resides in Philadelphia, PA.

> I would like to thank my friends and ex-coworkers, Ryan Macy and Jason Snowberger, for their feedback on this book and the editors who helped me refine the concepts and content of this book.

About the Reviewer

Ben Selby is a Software Engineer with a first class honors degree from Sheffield Hallam University and has over 8 years of commercial experience in software development. He has a passion for unit testable code, continuous integration, and software development processes utilizing automated quality assurance tools.

Over the past few years, Ben has contributed to open source software including phpDocumentor 2 (DocBlox), PHPUnit, PHP_CodeSniffer among others, and has authored three Sublime Text 2 plugins to aide PHP development.

www.packtpub.com

Support files, eBooks, discount offers and more

You might want to visit www.PacktPub.com for support files and downloads related to your book.

Did you know that Packt offers eBook versions of every book published, with PDF and ePub files available? You can upgrade to the eBook version at www.PacktPub.com and as a print book customer, you are entitled to a discount on the eBook copy. Get in touch with us at service@packtpub.com for more details.

At www.PacktPub.com, you can also read a collection of free technical articles, sign up for a range of free newsletters and receive exclusive discounts and offers on Packt books and eBooks.

packtLib.packtpub.com

Do you need instant solutions to your IT questions? PacktLib is Packt's online digital book library. Here, you can access, read and search across Packt's entire library of books.

Why Subscribe?

- Fully searchable across every book published by Packt
- Copy and paste, print and bookmark content
- On demand and accessible via web browser

Free Access for Packt account holders

If you have an account with Packt at www.PacktPub.com, you can use this to access PacktLib today and view nine entirely free books. Simply use your login credentials for immediate access.

Table of Contents

Instant Sublime Text Starter 1
So, what is Sublime Text 2? 3
Installation 4
OS X 4
Step 1 – Downloading Sublime Text 2 4
Step 2 – Installing 4
Step 3 – Launch 5
And that's it! 6
Ubuntu (Linux) 6
Step 1 – Download 64 bit or 32 bit? 6
Step 2 – Extract 7
Step 3 – Permissions 7
Step 4 – Launch 8
Step 5 – Add to user path (optional) 8
And that's it! 9
Windows 9
Step 1 – Download 64 bit or 32 bit? 9
Step 2 – Install 10
Step 3 – Launch 11
And that's it! 12
Quick start – Creating your first text document 13
Step 1 – Launch Sublime Text 2 13
Step 2 – Begin editing the file 14
Step 3 – Save the document 14
Quick start – Editing your first text document 15
Step 1 – Opening a document 15
Step 2 – Editing the file 16
Step 3 – Saving the file 16
Top features you need to know about 18
1 – Minimap 18
2 – Multiple cursors 19

Table of Contents

3 – Editor modes: Distraction Free and Vintage	19
Distraction Free mode	20
Vintage mode	20
4 – Goto Anything, Goto Symbol, and Goto Line	21
Goto Anything	21
Goto Symbol	22
Goto Line	23
5 – Command Palette	24
6 – Plugins using Package Control	24
Installing the Package Control plugin	24
Usage	25
Installing a package	26
Upgrading packages	26
Removing a package	27
7 – Snippets	27
8 – Macros	29
Assigning a hotkey	29
Example	30
People and places you should get to know	**32**
Official sites	32
Articles and tutorials	32
Community	32
Twitter	32

Instant Sublime Text Starter

Welcome to the *Instant Sublime Text Starter*. This book has been especially created to provide you with all the information that you need to start using the Sublime Text 2 text editor. You will learn the basics of how to install, customize, and utilize Sublime Text 2 and its rich feature set, including powerful navigation features, editing modes, and a rich plugin system.

This book contains the following sections:

So, what is Sublime Text 2? – In this section, learn what Sublime Text 2 is and how you can use it to be more productive.

Installation – In this section, learn how to install Sublime Text 2 on the three platforms it supports: Windows, OS X, and Linux. Also learn whether or not you need the 32-bit or 64-bit version.

Quick start – In this section, learn the basics of opening, editing, saving, the minimap, and the sidebar.

Top features you need to know about – In this section, learn about the minimap, multiple cursors, Goto Anything, Goto Symbol, and Goto Line, Distraction Free and Vintage modes, the Command Palette, and utilizing Package Control to manage your plugins.

People and places you should get to know – This section will get you started with Sublime Text 2, but there is plenty more to discover. This section will acquaint you with some useful sources of information regarding Sublime Text 2 including tutorials, the official blog and site, the unofficial documentation, and the Twitter feed of the author.

References – This section is an easy reference guide to various hotkeys and shortcuts used in Sublime Text 2 across different platforms. This section is not present in the book but is available as a free download from `http://www.packtpub.com/sites/default/files/downloads/3929OT_Appendix_3929OT_Sublime_Text_Starter_Micro.pdf`

So, what is Sublime Text 2?

Sublime Text 2 is the latest version of the popular text editor Sublime Text. It is a full-featured text editor great for editing local text files. It has many built-in features to aid in editing code, such as syntax highlighting, auto-indenting, file type recognition, a handy file/folder sidebar for easily editing of multiple files within a directory, macros to automate repetitious tasks, and tabs and a split-window option to view and edit multiple files at the same time. With Sublime Text 2's plethora of programmer-centric features, utilizing this editor can increase your productivity without bogging you down like full-fledged **Integrated Development Environments** (**IDE**) such as `Visual Studio` and `Eclipse`. These IDEs certainly have their place, but the simplicity of Sublime Text 2 can be preferable in other scenarios. In addition to the many useful built-in features, Sublime Text 2 was built from the ground up to be extensible and the Sublime Text community has taken note of it. Already, there are many useful extensions including interfaces for version control systems such as git, snippet packages for jQuery and PHP, and syntax highlighting for popular CSS wrapper languages such as LESS and SASS. Furthermore, the community has created Package Manager to make discovering, installing, updating, and managing these plugins as simple as typing a hotkey and a few characters. With a strong, configurable feature set and the ability to effortlessly extend Sublime Text 2, it can truly become your text editor and increase your productivity in the same way your tools should, while staying out of your way.

Installation

OS X

In three easy steps, you can install Sublime Text 2 on OS X and get it set up on your system. OS X Version 10.6+ is required.

Step 1 – Downloading Sublime Text 2

Navigate to `http://sublimetext.com/2`. Select the OS X version. Your download will begin immediately and will be saved wherever your browser is set to download files. By default, most browsers on OS X download to `~/Downloads`, which is accessible from the dock by default.

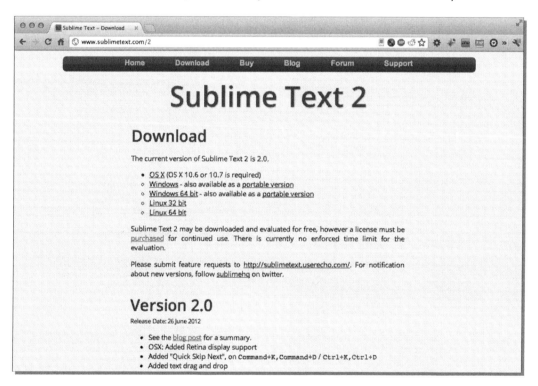

Step 2 – Installing

Double-click `SublimeText 2.0.1.dmg` in your download location to mount the disk image. Then drag the Sublime Text 2 bundle into the **Applications** folder shortcut in the disk image.

Instant Sublime Text Starter

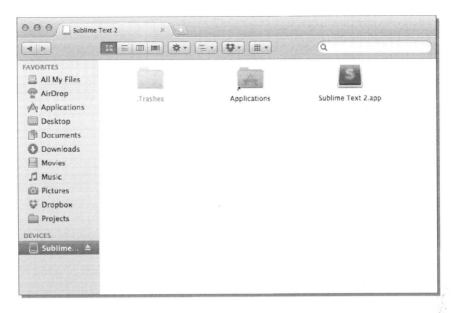

Step 3 – Launch

You can now launch Sublime Text 2 by navigating to your `Applications` folder or searching `Sublime Text 2` in Spotlight and launching from the results.

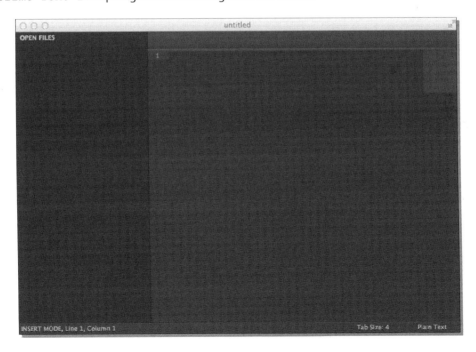

And that's it!

By this point, you should have a working installation of Sublime Text 2 on OS X and are free to play around and discover more.

Ubuntu (Linux)

In four or five easy steps you can install Sublime Text 2 on a Linux 64-bit or 32-bit system.

Step 1 – Download 64 bit or 32 bit?

Open a console and type `uname -m`. At this point you might see `x86_64` or `amd64` if you have a 64-bit operating system and an example 32-bit operating system output might be `i386`. Look up the output of `uname -m` if you are unsure which architecture you should download.

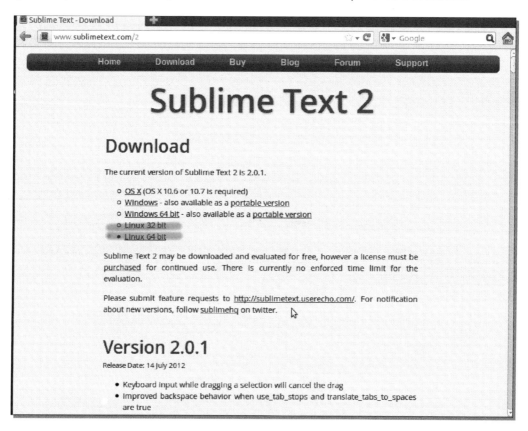

Step 2 – Extract

1. Once downloaded, navigate to your download location. By default, most browsers on Ubuntu download to `~/Downloads`.
2. Then extract the compressed file by typing `tar vxjf Sublime Text 2.0.1 x64.tar.bz2` for a 64-bit system or `tar vxjf Sublime Text 2.0.1.tar.bz2` for a 32-bit system.
3. Place the resulting folder wherever you put other user-installed applications (for example, `/usr/local/`).

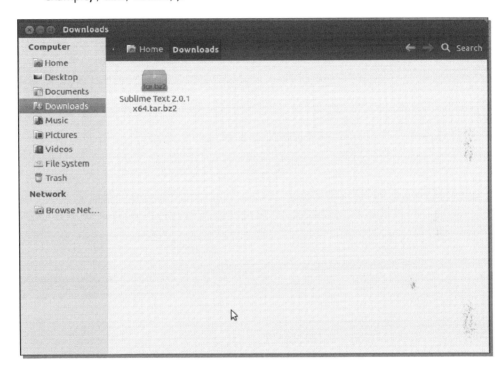

Step 3 – Permissions

To ensure that the `sublime_text` binary is executable, run the following command:

```
sudo chmod +x /path/to/sublime_text
```

At this point, you can execute `sublime_text` from the installation folder via your window manager or your command line. However, if you prefer, step 5, *Add to User Path (optional)*, will show you how to allow Sublime Text 2 to be executed from the command line anywhere on your system.

Step 4 – Launch

Navigate to the bin file `sublime_text` with either your window manager or your console and execute it.

Step 5 – Add to user path (optional)

In order to allow Sublime Text 2 to be executed from the command line (for example, `sublime_text my_text_file.txt`) from anywhere on the system, we must add the `sublime_text` binary to a location referenced by the `PATH` system variable. To do this, we will create a symbolic link in the `/usr/bin/` folder to the `sublime_text` binary by issuing the following command from the command line:

```
sudo ln -s /path/to/sublime_text /usr/bin/sublime_text
```

Additionally, the Sublime Text 2 binary file can be added to your environmental `PATH` variable to allow for command-line access without the need for symbolic links. To do so from bash, open `~/.bashrc` with your favorite text editor, and add `/path/to/sublime_text` to your `PATH` variable. If you are already setting your `PATH` variable, just add the path to the end. If you are not, add the following line:

```
PATH=$PATH:/path/to/sublime_text
```

And that's it!

By this point, you should have a working installation of Sublime Text 2 on Ubuntu and are free to play around and discover more.

Windows

In three easy steps you can install Sublime Text 2 on a Windows 64-bit or 32-bit system.

Step 1 – Download 64 bit or 32 bit?

Navigate to **Control Panel | System and Security | System**. Or you could right-click on **Computer** in the Start menu, or the icon for **Computer**, and select **Properties**. Once there, look under **System Type** where you will see either **32-bit Operating System** or **64-bit Operating System**. In the following screenshot, you will see that we are using a 64-bit operating system. Based on this information, download the appropriate version.

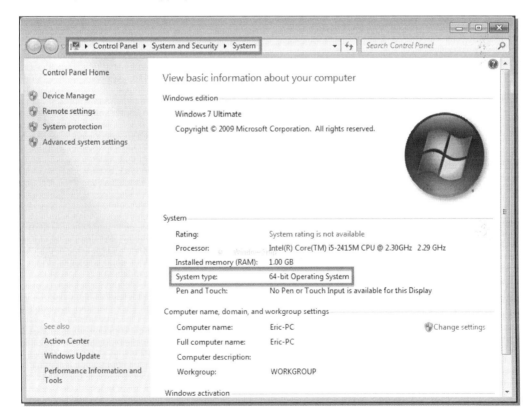

Instant Sublime Text Starter

After learning which Windows platform you are running, it's time to select that platform from the Sublime Text 2 Download page as shown in the following screenshot:

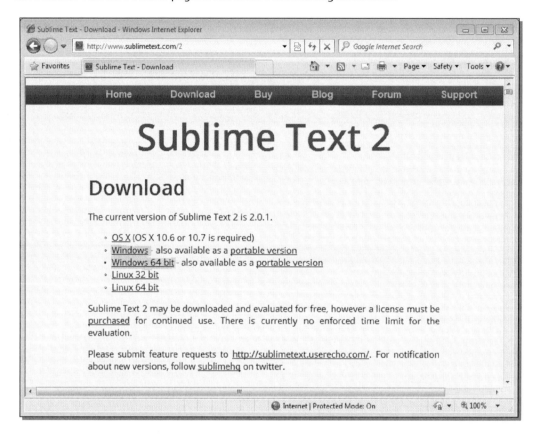

Step 2 – Install

Launch the setup from your download location. By default, Windows 7 downloads to the `Downloads` folder. Assuming your main hard drive is the `C:`, the path should be `C:\Users\YourUsername\Downloads`. If you are using a pre-Vista operating system (Windows XP or earlier), your path will be `C:\Documents and Settings\YourUsername\`. There is no default Downloads folder but downloads should default to `My Documents` unless changed. Follow the installation instructions to complete the Sublime Text 2 installation.

Instant Sublime Text Starter

Step 3 – Launch
You can find and launch **Sublime Text 2** from the Start menu under **All Programs**.

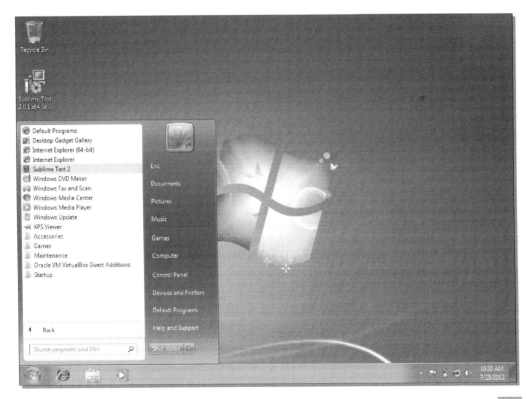

After selecting Sublime Text 2 from the Start menu, you should be presented with an instance of the editor, ready to go, as shown in the following screenshot:

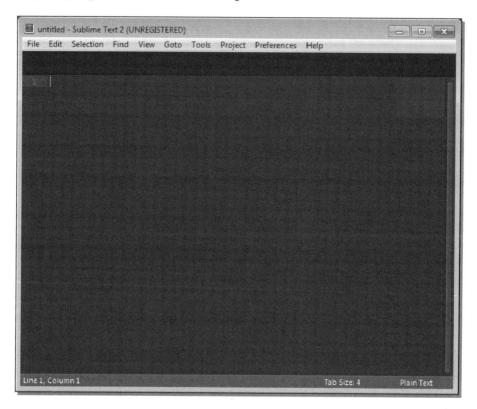

And that's it!

By this point, you should have a working installation of Sublime Text 2 on Windows and are free to play around and discover more.

Quick start – Creating your first text document

In this section we will briefly cover the task of creating a document and saving it.

Step 1 – Launch Sublime Text 2

Launch Sublime Text 2 in one of the ways referenced in the *Installation* section pertinent to your platform.

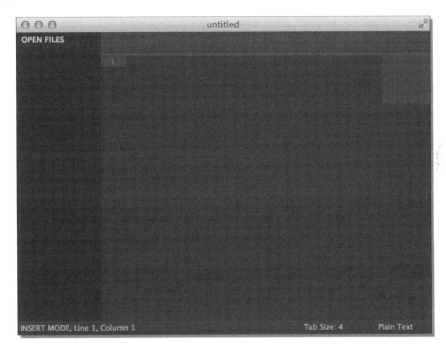

Step 2 – Begin editing the file

You can now begin typing your document. If you want to change the syntax of the file, which will highlight different keywords based on the language chosen, click on **Plain Text** in the bottom right-hand corner to be presented with a syntax menu as shown in the following screenshot:

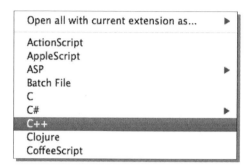

Step 3 – Save the document

When you are finished editing your file, it's time to save. You can click on **File | Save** or save the file using a hotkey. For OS X the hotkey is *command + S*. For all other platforms, the hotkey is *Ctrl + S*. The status bar along the bottom of the editor will change to alert you that the file has been saved.

Instant Sublime Text Starter

Quick start – Editing your first text document

This section covers how to edit an existing document.

Step 1 – Opening a document

1. Select **File | Open**.
2. Navigate to your files location and select the file.
3. Once the file is selected, click on **Open**.

You can also utilize the open file hotkey. For OS X the hotkey is *command + O*, and for all other platforms the command is *Ctrl + O*.

On Apple's OS X operating system, you can open a folder of files or a single file. On other platforms, there is a separate option in the **File** menu called **Open Folder...** for opening a folder.

Step 2 – Editing the file

You can then begin to edit the file. More features, such as the File Well for working with multiple files, multiline editing for making multiple simultaneous changes, and minimap for quickly navigating your document and seeing an overview, will be explained in the *Top features you need to know about* section.

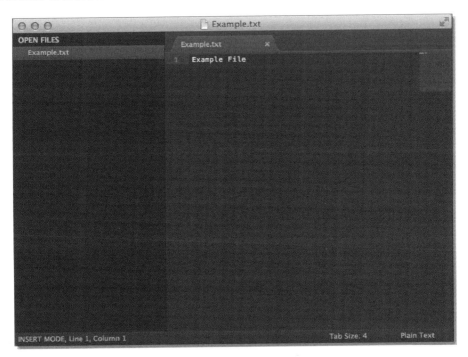

Step 3 – Saving the file

When you are finished editing your file, it's time to save. You can click on **File | Save** or save the file using a hotkey. For OS X the hotkey is *command + S*. For all other platforms, the hotkey is *Ctrl + S*. The status bar along the bottom of the editor will change to alert you that the file has been saved.

As mentioned before, the saved message will display in the status bar as noted in the following screenshot by the red outline:

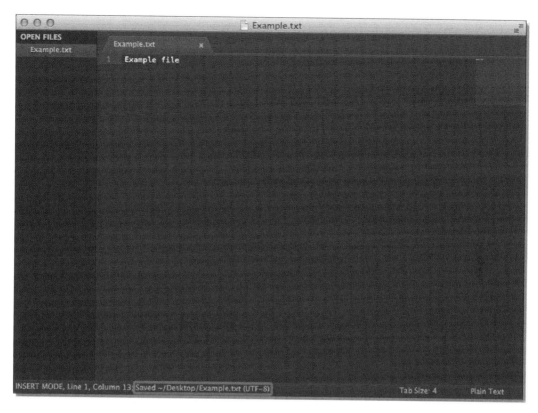

Top features you need to know about

At its core, Sublime Text 2 is a text editor. However, there are many features that make it stand out from the rest of the pack. These features include multiple cursors, a plugin system, and a few others which will be covered in this section.

1 – Minimap

The minimap is an innovative feature of Sublime Text 2 that gives you a bird's-eye view of the document you are editing. Always present at the right-hand side of the editor, it allows you to quickly look at a live, updated, zoomed out version of your current document. While the text will rarely be distinguishable, it allows for a topographical view of your document structure.

The minimap feature is also very useful for navigating a large document as it can behave similar to a scroll bar. When clicked on, the minimap can be used to scroll the document to a different portion.

However, should you find yourself not needing the minimap, or need the screen real estate it inhabits, it can easily be hidden by using the Menu bar to select **View | Hide Minimap**.

2 – Multiple cursors

Another way Sublime Text 2 differentiates itself from the crowded text editor market is by way of including the functionality that allows the user to edit a document in multiple places at the same time. This can be very useful when making an identical change in multiple places. It is especially useful when the change that needs to occur cannot be easily accomplished with find and replace. By pressing *command* + left-click on OS X, or *Ctrl* + left-click on other platforms, an additional cursor will be placed at the location of the click. Each additional cursor will mirror the original cursor.

The following screenshot shows a demo of this functionality. First, I created cursors on each of my three lines of text. Then I proceeded to type `test` without quotes:

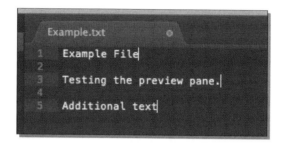

Now, as shown in the following screenshot, anything typed will be typed identically on the three lines where the cursors are placed. In this case I typed a space followed by the word `test`. This addition was simultaneous and I only had to make the change once, after creating the additional cursors.

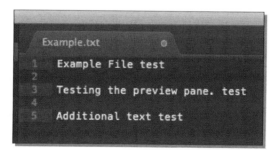

To return to a single cursor, simply press *Esc* or left-click anywhere on the document.

3 – Editor modes: Distraction Free and Vintage

Sublime Text 2 offers a couple of distinct modes. The first, **Distraction Free** mode, creates a simple interface for authoring/editing content. The second mode is the **Vintage** mode. This mode enables the editor to utilize many of the hotkeys as Vi/Vim and allows for moded editing. Both will be explained further in the following sections.

Distraction Free mode

Sublime Text 2 includes two modes that can modify the environment to possibly better suit your needs. The first, Distraction Free, is a welcome mode for simple authoring of text. When in Distraction Free mode, the editor not only takes up the entire screen but removes the File Well at the left, the status bar at the bottom, the menu bar at the top, and the minimap at the right. Distraction Free mode can be entered by pressing *Ctrl + Shift + command + F* on OS X or *Ctrl + Shift* + Super (Windows key) + *F*.

```
Example file test

Demonstrating the distraction free mode.

Lorem ipsum dolor sit amet, consectetur adipiscing elit. Aliquam lacinia
malesuada purus, nec bibendum nisi commodo ac. Sed a neque ac sem iaculis
adipiscing sed at tortor. Donec id semper mauris. Mauris quis placerat velit.
Sed et pharetra nunc. Duis sagittis euismod dolor. In vel tincidunt ligula.
Integer a lacus a nisi bibendum accumsan. Maecenas non adipiscing orci.
Aliquam euismod, sem in venenatis lobortis, nibh quam vehicula orci, vel
rhoncus lacus mauris a dui. Fusce commodo auctor aliquet. Nulla facilisi.
Vivamus non ligula faucibus metus sollicitudin ultrices. Ut et adipiscing purus
.
Praesent id nibh ac ligula tempus malesuada non at massa. Nunc vel lacus tellus
. Donec facilisis nulla vel nulla fermentum consequat. Aenean sit amet auctor
erat. Donec bibendum neque eget ante pretium id porttitor felis bibendum.
Vestibulum tortor eros, mattis a elementum quis, faucibus non magna. Donec et
urna mi. Phasellus eget mauris ac velit semper placerat et at odio. Integer
ultrices lacinia justo, sollicitudin bibendum libero auctor a. Nam eget quam
neque. Ut molestie cursus nunc ut dapibus. Quisque mattis porta ligula, nec
commodo ligula luctus ut. Sed id nisi sit amet velit vulputate commodo. Sed
hendrerit mi at turpis condimentum aliquam. Nunc at tortor nibh, sagittis
facilisis nisl.

Vivamus in tortor vel mi pretium elementum sit amet vitae odio. Praesent
bibendum dui vel augue cursus lobortis. Maecenas nibh nibh, posuere nec
tristique et, feugiat vehicula dolor. Duis id sapien tristique dolor
condimentum interdum. In hac habitasse platea dictumst. In et metus quis risus
venenatis pulvinar. Cras sed felis ligula. Donec lacinia ante quis nisl
ultrices interdum. Etiam sodales ipsum a justo bibendum lacinia.

Proin in lectus id diam lobortis porttitor eget vel nibh. Pellentesque posuere
dui ut diam ultrices ac egestas tellus molestie. In ullamcorper tempor sagittis
. Sed a accumsan nisl. Etiam tincidunt urna in magna feugiat sit amet volutpat
turpis eleifend. Nullam quis sem lectus, vel rhoncus est. Vestibulum viverra
sapien nec eros cursus sollicitudin. Aliquam lacus sem, interdum sed mattis
quis, eleifend vitae libero.
```

Vintage mode

Vintage mode, aka Vi-Mode, adds moded editing. If you have no experience with a moded editor such as Vi or Vim, you will probably not want to enable this mode. In effect, this mode adds basic command and insert modes from the popular Vi/Vim editors. A large subset of Vi/Vim hotkeys are available by default and, via the VintageEx plugin, support for additional Vi/Vim hotkeys can be added. The following steps detail how to enable Vintage mode:

1. Select **Preferences | Settings – Default**. Edit the `ignored_packages` setting, changing it from `"ignored_packages": ["Vintage"]` to `"ignored_packages": []`.

2. Save the file. Sublime Text 2 now uses Vintage mode. At the bottom of the editor, in the status line, you should see **INSERT MODE**.

> INSERT MODE, Line 1, Column 22

3. Pressing *Esc* will put you in command mode and the status line should reflect that as well as your cursor.
4. Once in command mode, pressing *I* will return you to insert mode.

For additional information, navigate to `http://www.sublimetext.com/docs/2/vintage.html`.

4 – Goto Anything, Goto Symbol, and Goto Line

Sublime Text 2 makes it easy to navigate your projects and files with various Goto features. These will be described in more detail in the following sections.

Goto Anything

Goto Anything allows the user to display any open file quickly. By pressing *command + P* on OS X, or *Ctrl + P* on other platforms, a dialog will display a list of open files, including any files in a directory or subdirectory that was opened. This allows you to fuzzy search for a filename of any file. It can also be invoked from the **Goto** menu item. Goto Anything is especially helpful when utilizing a framework with many directories and files such as Ruby on Rails.

Once invoked, as you type, your search parameters will narrow the list of files.

As the following screenshot shows, a fuzzy search was performed in both open files and the contents of the file itself:

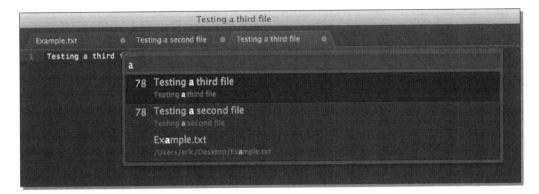

You can also quickly dig into a specific open directory by simply fuzzy searching with directory separators (/ for OS X and Linux, \ for Windows).

In the preceding example, I was able to easily restrict my search to the `views` folder located inside the `app` folder by simply typing a portion of the folder followed by a directory separator.

Goto Symbol

Goto Symbol allows for fuzzy searching of symbols such as defined functions. Goto Symbol can be invoked via *command + R* on OS X, *Ctrl + R* on other platforms, from under the **Goto** menu item, or by invoking Goto Anything and typing @ (an at symbol, *Shift + 2*).

Goto Line

Navigating to any line in the currently open file is as easy as hitting *Ctrl + G* on all three supported platforms, or invoking Goto Line from under the **Goto** menu item, or typing : (colon) while in Goto Anything.

Instant Sublime Text Starter

5 – Command Palette

Sublime Text 2 allows for many of its commands to be executed without ever leaving the keyboard via the Command Palette. To invoke the Command Palette, press *command + Shift + P* on OS X, *Ctrl + Shift + P* on other platforms, or under the **Tools** menu item.

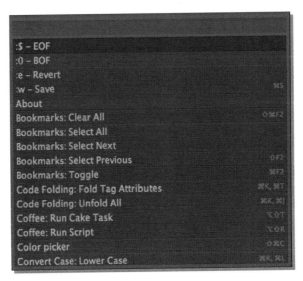

As the following screenshot shows, a fuzzy search is performed on available commands:

As with the other similar menus, this search is fuzzy as well. From here, you can invoke a number of commands.

6 – Plugins using Package Control

Sublime Text 2 was written from the ground up to be extensible. As a user, you can install plugins manually, or utilize Package Control. I highly recommend utilizing Package Control for managing your Sublime Text 2 plugins and will detail how to do so now.

Installing the Package Control plugin

1. Open the Sublime Text 2 console by pressing *Ctrl + '* (control plus backtick).

2. Type the following Python script into the console to automatically install Package Control:

```
import urllib2,os; pf='Package Control.sublime-package';
ipp=sublime.installed_packages_path(); os.makedirs(ipp) if not
os.path.exists(ipp) else None; urllib2.install_opener(urllib2.
build_opener(urllib2.ProxyHandler())); open(os.path.
join(ipp,pf),'wb').write(urllib2.urlopen('http://sublime.wbond.
net/'+pf.replace(' ','%20')).read()); print 'Please restart
Sublime Text to finish installation'
```

That is a large amount of text to type out manually. I recommend navigating to the creator's website and viewing the installation instructions. There you can copy and paste the script. The website is: `http://wbond.net/sublime_packages/package_control/installation`.

3. Restart Sublime Text 2 and you now have Package Control installed.

You can also manually install Package Control with the following steps:

1. Click on **Preferences | Browse Packages...**.
2. Navigate up one directory and then to the `Installed Packages` folder.
3. Download the Package Control package from the wbond website `http://sublime.wbond.net/Package%20Control.sublime-package`.
4. Copy the package into the `Installed Packages` folder.
5. Restart Sublime Text 2 and you now have Package Control installed.

Usage

Package Control is installed as a Sublime Text 2 command. This means it is easily accessed via the Command Palette detailed previously. Once in the Command Palette, typing `Package Control:` will limit the choices to only the Package Control options shown in the following screenshot:

```
Package Control:
Package Control: Add Channel
Package Control: Add Repository
Package Control: Disable Package
Package Control: Discover Packages
Package Control: Enable Package
Package Control: Install Package
Package Control: List Packages
Package Control: Remove Package
Package Control: Upgrade Package
Package Control: Create Package File
Package Control: Create Binary Package File
Package Control: Upgrade/Overwrite All Packages
```

For the sake of brevity, we will just cover how to install, update, and remove packages. Some items are self-explanatory and others are beyond the scope of this book.

Installing a package

Selecting **Install Package** will bring up a list of available packages included with the default channel.

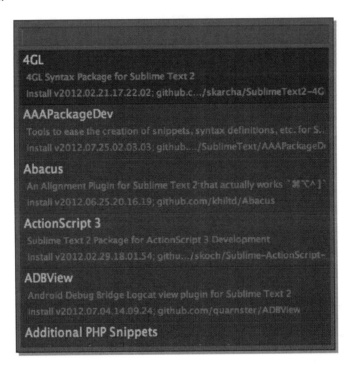

Selecting a package will install that package. Each package is a little different and you will need to examine their README files in order to see how to configure and use the particular plugin in question. The easiest way to do this is via the **Package Control: List Packages** item in the Command Palette. Once selected, search for the package in question and hit *Enter*. This will open the folder containing the package where the README is most likely located.

Upgrading packages

The **Upgrade Package** and **Upgrade/Overwrite All Packages** options are relatively self-explanatory. When selected, the **Upgrade Package** option will allow you to select a single package to update. The **Upgrade/Overwrite All Packages** option updates all the installed packages. Additionally, Package Control's settings file can be modified to automatically upgrade packages by setting the `auto_upgrade` equal to `true`.

Removing a package

This option is also relatively self-documenting. Once selected, you will be presented with a list of installed packages. Selecting a package will remove it from your installed packages.

7 – Snippets

Sublime Text 2 includes a snippets feature allowing you to define tab-activated triggers to expand text. To create your own text snippets, follow these steps:

1. Click on **Tools | New Snippet…**.

2. You will be presented with the default snippet and some tips as follows:

   ```
   <snippet>
     <content><![CDATA[
   Hello, ${1:this} is a ${2:snippet}.
   ]]></content>
     <!-- Optional: Set a tabTrigger to define how to trigger the snippet -->
     <!-- <tabTrigger>hello</tabTrigger> -->
     <!-- Optional: Set a scope to limit where the snippet will trigger -->
     <!-- <scope>source.python</scope> -->
   </snippet>
   ```

3. After saving the snippet it is now accessible via the **Snippets…** menu item in **Tools** and via the Command Palette accessible via the *command* + *Shift* + *P* on OS X or *Ctrl* + *Shift* + *P* on other platforms. However, in order to invoke the snippet via tab activation, you must set a "tab trigger". A tab trigger is the string of text that is typed followed by hitting the *Tab* key replacing the trigger with your snippet. The following is a sample snippet that automates a useful debugging string in HTML with PHP:

   ```
   <snippet>
     <content><![CDATA[
   die("<pre>" . print_r($${1:array}, 1) . "</pre>");
   ]]></content>
     <!-- Optional: Set a tabTrigger to define how to trigger the snippet -->
     <tabTrigger>dppr</tabTrigger>
     <!-- Optional: Set a scope to limit where the snippet will trigger -->
     <scope>source.php</scope>
   </snippet>
   ```

First, we'll look at this snippet in action, and then we will discuss the syntax. First we type `dppr`; I made this my tab trigger as it stands for "die pre print_r", which is a debugging snippet I use regularly to inspect the contents of a PHP array by essentially printing it to the browser in a readable format.

Next we hit *Tab* while our cursor is still adjacent to the last character of our tab trigger to expand our trigger into our snippet.

Notice the array portion of the line is already selected for us because we wrapped `array` in the dollar and curly braces `${1:array}`. That tells Sublime Text 2 to select that portion of the snippet first. Had we had another item denoted by `${2:anotherArray}`, once we completed modifying `array`, we could just hit *Tab* again to move onto the next item, in this example `anotherArray`.

While this is a real snippet I personally employ, the actual contents of this particular snippet are not important. What is important is realizing how much time and typing this feature can save you. Snippets can be much simpler or much more complicated than this. For instance, if you find yourself typing your e-mail address or maybe your home address out a lot, you could create a snippet with a tab trigger of `email` that expands to `myemail@domain.com` or `addr` that expands to your home address. An example of a more complicated snippet might be the structure of a default HTML page (that is, the `html`, `head`, `title`, and `body` tags) along with multiple tab stops for creating the title and dropping your cursor into the body element. In fact, Sublime Text 2 has that exact snippet with a tab trigger of `html`.

8 – Macros

Sublime Text 2 allows you to automate repetitive tasks with recordable macros. To create a macro, follow these steps:

1. Click on **Tools** | **Record Macro**, or you can hit *Ctrl + Q*.
2. Walk through any actions you wish to automate. Keep in mind that any actions taken here need to be general to the type of scenario you wish to automate. For instance, when moving to the end or beginning of a line, use the hotkey to do so instead of pressing the arrow keys a certain number of times. This allows the macro to work on any length of line.
3. Once finished with your actions, click on **Tools** | **Stop Record Macro** or hit *Ctrl + Q* again.

At this point, you now have a macro, but it is not saved anywhere. You can choose to play back the macro by hitting **Tools** | **Playback Macro** or by hitting *Ctrl + Shift + Q*. Or, if you would like to save the macro, click on **Tools** | **Save Macro** and give your macro file a name ending in `.sublime-macro`. At this point you can now access the macro by navigating to **Tools** | **Macros** | *Your macro*. However, you may want to save yourself the clicks by assigning a hotkey. In the next section, we explore how to do exactly that.

Assigning a hotkey

After saving your macro, assign a hotkey by following these steps:

1. On OS X click on **Sublime Text 2** | **Preferences** | **Key Bindings - User** or on other platforms, hit **Preferences** | **Key Bindings – User**.
2. Once the file is open we can add our hotkey.
3. All of Sublime Text 2's preference files are in the JSON format and hotkeys are no different.

4. The format of a Sublime Text 2 hotkey is as follows; anything surrounded by less-than and greater-than signs (<>) needs to be replaced with your information but anything else is required:

```
{ "keys": ["<hotkey here>"], "command": "run_macro_file", "args":
{ "file": "<path to your macro file ending in .sublime-macro" } }
```

A comprehensive list of available key names can be found in the unofficial Sublime Text 2 documentation. A link can be found in the "People and places you should get to know" section. The following screenshot shows my example:

Note a couple things from the preceding screenshot. First, I saved my macro in the default location brought up when my macro was saved. (In this case, a Unix-style path. A Windows path would have backslashes instead of forward slashes). Secondly, when I saved my macro, I named it `EOLSemicolon.sublime-macro`, and this is the file referenced at the end of the path. Finally, notice I already had a user-defined hotkey that I needed to place a comma after (specifically after the final right curly-brace, }) in order to separate it from my previous hotkey designation.

5. At this point, save the file as you would save any other text file. If there are any syntax errors in your hotkey file, you will be alerted with a popup.

6. Sublime Text 2 automatically updates after many changes, and this is one of them. After saving the file, the hotkey and macro should be available.

Example

Now that you know how to use a macro, let's look at a simple example of where one might be useful.

In the following section, we explore how to add a semicolon to the end of any line from anywhere on that line. This could be useful for terminating the following line of PHP after typing the parameter:

```
<?php
  mysql_real_escape_string("'; Drop Table users;")
?>
```

While only a minor inconvenience, multiply this over a large file with many function calls, and the keystrokes add up. We can remove one keystroke and make it easy to add that semicolon.

So, with our cursor anywhere on the line, proceed with the following steps:

1. Press *Ctrl + Q* to begin recording a macro.
2. Press the hotkey to move to the end of the line, *command* + right-arrow on OS X or *Ctrl* + right-arrow on other platforms.
3. Press semicolon (;).
4. Press *Ctrl + Q* to stop recording the macro.

After saving the macro and defining a hotkey in the manner described in previous sections, press the hotkey anywhere on a line you would like to end with a semicolon.

People and places you should get to know

If you need help with Sublime Text 2 or just want to learn more, here are some people and places which will prove invaluable.

Official sites

- **Homepage**: http://www.sublimetext.com/2
- **Manual and documentation**: http://www.sublimetext.com/docs/2/
- **Support**: http://www.sublimetext.com/support
- **Blog**: http://www.sublimetext.com/blog/
- **Twitter**: https://twitter.com/#!/sublimehq

Articles and tutorials

- **A great getting started guide**: http://opensoul.org/blog/archives/2012/01/12/getting-started-with-sublime-text-2/
- **Some good tips and tricks**: http://net.tutsplus.com/tutorials/tools-and-tips/sublime-text-2-tips-and-tricks/
- **Some great tips for beginners**: http://blog.alainmeier.com/post/27255145114/some-things-beginners-might-not-know-about-sublime-text
- **Three months with Sublime Text 2**: http://steverandytantra.com/thoughts/three-months-with-sublime-text-2

Community

- **Official forums**: http://www.sublimetext.com/forum/
- **Feature requests**: http://sublimetext.userecho.com/
- **Unofficial documentation**: http://docs.sublimetext.info/en/latest/index.html
- **Sales FAQ**: http://www.sublimetext.com/sales_faq

Twitter

- **Sublime Text 2 Tips on Twitter**: https://twitter.com/sublimetips
- **Package Control on Twitter**: https://twitter.com/ST2PkgControl

For more open source information, follow Packt Publishing at @packtopensource.

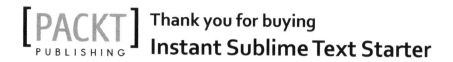

Thank you for buying
Instant Sublime Text Starter

About Packt Publishing

Packt, pronounced 'packed', published its first book "*Mastering phpMyAdmin for Effective MySQL Management*" in April 2004 and subsequently continued to specialize in publishing highly focused books on specific technologies and solutions.

Our books and publications share the experiences of your fellow IT professionals in adapting and customizing today's systems, applications, and frameworks. Our solution based books give you the knowledge and power to customize the software and technologies you're using to get the job done. Packt books are more specific and less general than the IT books you have seen in the past. Our unique business model allows us to bring you more focused information, giving you more of what you need to know, and less of what you don't.

Packt is a modern, yet unique publishing company, which focuses on producing quality, cutting-edge books for communities of developers, administrators, and newbies alike. For more information, please visit our website: www.packtpub.com.

Writing for Packt

We welcome all inquiries from people who are interested in authoring. Book proposals should be sent to author@packtpub.com. If your book idea is still at an early stage and you would like to discuss it first before writing a formal book proposal, contact us; one of our commissioning editors will get in touch with you.

We're not just looking for published authors; if you have strong technical skills but no writing experience, our experienced editors can help you develop a writing career, or simply get some additional reward for your expertise.

TextMate How-To

ISBN: 978-1-84969-398-1   Paperback: 76 pages

Over 20 fast and furious timesaving recipes for using TextMate efficiency and effectively

1. Hit the ground running using the powerfully versatile text and code editor — TextMate from Macromates
2. Attention on keyboard shortcuts and multiple routes to actions to satisfy anyone's preferred coding style
3. Installing and use several extremely helpful bundles such as Todo, Zen Coding, Markdown, and more

Python 2.6 Text Processing: Beginners Guide

ISBN: 978-1-84951-212-1   Paperback: 380 pages

The easiest way to learn how to manipulate text with Python

1. The easiest way to learn text processing with Python
2. Deals with the most important textual data formats you will encounter
3. Learn to use the most popular text processing libraries available for Python
4. Packed with examples to guide you through

Please check **www.PacktPub.com** for information on our titles

Microsoft Silverlight 4 Data and Services Cookbook

ISBN: 978-1-84719-984-3   Paperback: 476 pages

Over 85 practical recipes for creating rich, data-driven business applications in Silverlight

1. Design and develop rich data-driven business applications in Silverlight
2. Rapidly interact with and handle multiple sources of data and services within Silverlight business applications
3. Silverlight business applications by binding data to Silverlight controls, validating data in Silverlight, getting data from services into Silverlight applications and much more!

Hacking Vim 7.2

ISBN: 978-1-84951-050-9   Paperback: 244 pages

Ready-to-use hacks with solutions for common situations encountered by users of the Vim editor

1. Create, install, and use Vim scripts to extend Vim's functionality
2. Personalize your work-area to fit your workflow
3. Optimize your Vim editor to be faster and more responsive
4. Packed with tips and tricks based on the author's practical experience

Please check **www.PacktPub.com** for information on our titles

Made in the USA
Lexington, KY
14 January 2015